Original title:
In the Orchard's Light

Copyright © 2025 Creative Arts Management OÜ
All rights reserved.

Author: Isabella Rosemont
ISBN HARDBACK: 978-1-80586-323-6
ISBN PAPERBACK: 978-1-80586-795-1

The Lifeline of Gnarled Trunks

Beneath the branches, squirrels prance,
Dodging apples in a silly dance.
Old trunks gossip, bark as a crew,
While ladybugs form a conga queue.

Weathered limbs hold tales so grand,
Of fruit that never took a stand.
Cranky owls mock the bumblebee,
Who dreams of honey, oh! Let her be!

Flickers of Eternal Spring

The blooms debate which shade is best,
Pink or white? They jostle, jest.
Bees are fashionably late, oh dear,
While butterflies laugh and cheer.

Frogs leap by in rainbow tights,
Joining in on the silly flights.
Daffodils giggle in the breeze,
Sharing secrets with the trees.

Blushing Fruits of Promise

Cherries blush, in a fruit parade,
Who wore what? A fruity charade.
Peaches gossip, "Have you heard?"
While plums mime, quite absurd!

The elderberries offer advice,
"Add some sugar, it's very nice!"
But too much talk can make them pout,
Guess what? They might just go without!

A Gathering of Seasons' Colors

Autumn laughs in a vibrant mood,
Dancing with leaves, all bright and rude.
Winter chuckles, "Let's have a chill!"
With snowflakes joking, "Time to spill!"

Spring jumps in with a wild fling,
Bringing warmth and a funny zing.
Summer sighs, "Oh, what a scene!"
In the chaos, who knows what's clean?

Leaves Like Laughter

Rustling whispers, trees conspire,
Gossiping leaves, all they require.
A squirrel slips, does a comical twirl,
Nature's own jester, giving it a whirl.

Giggling branches, playful and spry,
Tickling breeze makes the branches sigh.
Fruits dangle low, a cheeky display,
"Pick me!" they shout, in a fruity ballet.

The Morning's Golden Glimmer

Sunrise stretches with a sleepy yawn,
The rooster crows, 'Come on, let's fawn!'
Crispy toast sings in the kitchen heat,
While coffee's aroma dances on the street.

Bubbly laughter spills, a friendly tease,
As pancakes flip with utmost ease.
Golden syrup flows like jokes in the air,
A morning so bright, who could despair?

Rippled Reflections in the Dew

Morning dew, beads of bright fun,
Each droplet shines like laughter run.
A frog leaps high to catch a sunbeam,
With a splat in the pond, he's the joke's theme!

Ripples giggle, jump and jibe,
As fish splash in, enhancing the vibe.
They share giggles beneath leafy shades,
While sunlight dapples like playful charades.

The Dance of Bees and Blossoms

Bees buzz about, with tiny top hats,
Waltzing 'round flowers, they're all like acrobats!
Petals pretend to be shy and coy,
But they fling open, inviting joy.

A bumbling bee trips, lands on a bloom,
With a comedic flair, he finds his room.
Bees and blooms, a merry affair,
Nature's own gala, beyond compare!

Sanctuary of Solitude.

In a place where apples fall,
A squirrel's dance, a funny call.
Chasing shadows, hopping fast,
Who knew fruit could make one laugh?

Bright lemons rolling down the lane,
Dodging bees, a silly game.
Bananas wearing tiny hats,
Oh, the sight of goofy chats!

Whispers Among the Blossoms

Petals giggle in the breeze,
Telling jokes to buzzing bees.
A funny tune from trees so tall,
Echoing laughter, a fruity sprawl.

The cherries blush as they tease,
"Catch me quick, or you'll just freeze!"
Peaches grinning, one and all,
While plums bump into the garden wall.

Sunlit Canopy Dreams

Underneath a shady dome,
The birds claim it as their home.
Chickens scratch and start to cluck,
Finding humor in their luck.

The sunlight winks, a playful glance,
Encouraging all to dance.
A rabbit twirls, a comical sight,
While veggies cheer with pure delight!

Beneath the Fruitful Boughs

Beneath the branches, shadows swing,
A jester's hat on a daffodil's ring.
Grapes gather round for a jest,
Joking about who's the very best.

Hilarious tales of flying seeds,
Spreading laughter like wild weeds.
A melon rolls, and everyone shouts,
"Looks like we've got some epic clouts!"

Sun-drenched Whispers

Beneath the sun, the apples grin,
They giggle loud, they spin and spin.
A pear dressed up in fancy wear,
Winks at the clouds, without a care.

Squirrels chat and trade their nuts,
While bees debate in silly huddles.
A rogue red robin, bright and spry,
Sings off-key to the blushing sky.

Harvest of Dreams

Pumpkins plotting tricks and schemes,
Dance in potions of their dreams.
The corn stalks wave, but that's quite rude,
They sent a scarecrow out for food.

Dandelions start a cheerleading crew,
Puffing clouds like it's a debut.
Lemons laugh when life gets sour,
Turning frowns into a shower.

Stars Sprinkle Over Saplings

Little sprouts with twinkling eyes,
Dream of reaching up to the skies.
A moonlit joke, a comet's laugh,
Tickles roots in grassy paths.

Crickets play their tiny strings,
While giggling leaves dance in rings.
Fireflies blink in syncopation,
Creating a nighttime celebration.

Beneath the Canopy's Watchful Eye

Under branches, mischief brews,
Ducks in hats playing at the zoo.
A shy snail slides with grand aplomb,
While roguish rabbits plot a bomb.

The wise old owl, with laughter hoots,
Solicits wisdom from the roots.
In tangled vines, the laughter twirls,
As nature spins her playful pearls.

Glimmers of Past and Present

Beneath the branches, laughter rings,
A squirrel plays, and mischief springs.
Old tales whisper through the leaves,
While butterflies dance, as if to tease.

Time's tick-tock wears a funny hat,
With a wink and a nod, not one tit for tat.
We share a joke with the buzzing bees,
And giggle together at a playful breeze.

Nature's Gilded Canvas

Colors explode like confetti tossed,
Yet the crow squawks as if he's lost.
A palette bright, but watch your step,
For muddy boots are nature's prep!

The sun paints smiles on every fruit,
While worms wiggle in a jolly pursuit.
Nature's brush has a sense of flair,
Even daisies wear their funny hair.

The Heartbeat of Earth

An acorn drops with a thud and roll,
As if auditioning for a comedic role.
The grass giggles with each playful sway,
And ants march on in a silly ballet.

The wind tells jokes in a rustling tone,
While bunnies hop like they're on loan.
Each vagrant cloud drifts slow and sly,
As if to tease the watchful sky.

Dancing Shadows on Soft Soil

In the playful shadows, quirks collide,
Where bumblebees buzz with pride.
A sunlight jig, a moonlit twist,
Even the daisies can't resist!

Footprints prance, a slapstick song,
As crickets chirp with a cheeky throng.
Under the canopy of silly trees,
Nature laughs along in joyful tease.

Fruits of Solitude

Apples dance on tree tops high,
While bananas giggle, oh my!
Pears wear hats, they think it's neat,
Trading fruit jokes, quite the feat.

Cherries plot to steal the show,
Citrus peels all start to flow.
Lemons laugh at sour news,
While grapes sip tea, they can't lose.

Radiant Roots

Carrots in a shy parade,
Showing off their leafy braid.
Radishes with rosy cheeks,
Whisper loud, no need for sneaks.

Potatoes in a denim mood,
Sway and shuffle, oh so crude!
Beetroot blushes deep and red,
As turnips dance, they take the lead.

Hidden Stories

Underneath the leafy shade,
Stories of adventure laid.
Rabbits laugh, the crickets sing,
As squirrels tease with nutty bling.

The lost pear tells a fable sweet,
Of mishaps in a race with beet.
Lemons giggle, tales unfold,
In hidden spots where fruit is bold.

Echoes of a Child's Laughter

Oranges bounce like little kids,
While strawberries play hide and bids.
Kiwi sings a silly tune,
Underneath the bright round moon.

Watermelons roll with glee,
In a game of hide and flee.
Grapes drop jokes, the crowd erupts,
As fruit-filled laughter interrupts.

Seeds of Tomorrow's Sky

Seeds spread stories on the breeze,
They talk of dreams with such great ease.
Tomatoes giggle, full of cheer,
Wishing on the clouds so near.

Pumpkins wish to hug the sun,
Spreading joy, oh what fun!
With each sprout, a laugh erupts,
In fields where laughter loudly thumps.

Flickering Fireflies in the Twilight

The fireflies dance with a giggle,
Their glow makes the frogs start to wiggle.
A squeaky mouse joins in the ballet,
While owls hoot jokes that are quite cliché.

In the dusk, the crickets join the fun,
Singing in harmony, one by one.
The sun hands out its last golden cheer,
As squirrels play hide and seek without fear.

The raccoons wear masks like it's Halloween,
Stealing snacks, they're a sneaky scene.
Underneath the stars, the laughter grows,
As the night spins tales that nobody knows.

But wait, what's that? A cat with a hat?
Trying to catch fireflies with a spat.
He trips and tumbles, oh what a sight!
Flickering fireflies just laugh with delight.

Fleeting Days Beneath a Blossoming Sky

A bumblebee buzzes with glee,
Over flowers drinking sweet tea.
The petals sway like they're at a dance,
While ants parade in a tiny romance.

With every breeze, giggles erupt,
As daisies whisper, "Hey, what's up?"
A butterfly winks with colorful grace,
Playing hide and seek in a pollen race.

Days flicker on as shadows grow long,
Squirrels rehearse their acorn song.
A lizard flips like it's on a roll,
While kids chase butterflies for a stroll.

The sun dips low with a silly grin,
Casting gold on the chaos within.
As laughter peeks from behind the trees,
The fleeting days dance on a warm breeze.

Sun-Kissed Branches

Sunshine dances on the leaves,
Apples giggle in the breeze.
Chasing bees in silly games,
Lemons laugh and call us names.

Squirrels steal a berry's crown,
While a pear rolls down the town.
Cherries munch on their own pies,
As plums plot all their sweet lies.

A rascal vine trips a shy peach,
"Watch your step!" the branches teach.
Coconuts drop with a thud,
Adding to our fruit-filled mud.

In a patch of grassy cheer,
We toast to the fruits we hold dear.
Life's a laugh, so come and play,
In our sunny, fruity ballet.

Whispering Fruits

Bananas gossip in a row,
Telling tales that make us glow.
Berries whisper sweet secrets low,
While grapes play tag, then in a tow.

A cucumber wigs out in shock,
As pickles join the fruit-a-hock.
"Wait for me!" the melons shriek,
While pumpkins dance, so bold and cheek.

Kiwis crack jokes about their fuzz,
And lemons cheer, "This is the buzz!"
We giggle under leafy shade,
As fruits throw jokes, their plans cascade.

With laughter ripe, we toast again,
To fruits of humor, come join in!
A silly feast we can't outrun,
In this garden of fruity fun.

Shadows Beneath the Boughs

Under shadows, laughter grows,
Tomatoes wear their prison clothes.
A radish rolls, a carrot grins,
While peppers play at growing fins.

The melon crew juggles well,
A kernel's dance, it's quite the spell.
Onions make a stinky scene,
Faltering like a clumsy queen.

Lettuce whispers, "Don't be shy,"
Bouncing beans leap up to fly.
Radishes laugh in rosy tones,
As broccoli cracks up with groans.

Underneath this leafy roof,
We share our jokes and humor's proof.
So gather round, your fears dismiss,
Beneath the boughs, you'll find your bliss.

Twilight's Harvest

Beneath the glow of fading light,
Gardens hum with pure delight.
Corn holds court, with ears so wise,
As peppers share their goofy lies.

Vines are tangled with their cheer,
While pumpkins pivot, shedding fear.
Tomatoes spin a silly yarn,
And carrots dance without a barn.

"Look at me!" a potato shouts,
"I'm a rock star, no doubts!"
But then he trips on his own sprout,
And all the veggies yell and clout.

As twilight brings the giggle spree,
We harvest jokes as light runs free.
So gather 'round, the day is done,
In twilight's warmth, we've surely won.

Whispered Secrets of the Saplings

Little leaves giggle in a breeze,
Branching out, they talk with ease.
Silly bugs dance on the ground,
In their world, laughter knows no bound.

Roots make puns beneath the soil,
Tickled by worms that love to toil.
A squirrel cracks jokes 'bout the trees,
While shadows whisper with a tease.

A sunbeam rolls and starts to play,
Chasing droplets on their way.
Petals blush at the joyful sound,
As the earth spins round and round.

Oh, to be young with laughter shared,
In nature's arms, all souls are bared.
Saplings chuckle, their joy unmeasured,
In secret peace, where laughter's treasured.

Nature's Embrace After Rain

Raindrops tickle the leaves on high,
Splashes of joy as puddles sigh.
Worms don tiny hats made of dew,
Playing dress-up like fools would do.

Sunflowers stretch with a yawn so wide,
While grass blades laugh on every side.
Frogs croon songs with a croaky cheer,
Their little concerts bring all to hear.

Clouds critique the rainbow's glow,
Saying, 'Too violet! Let's tone it low.'
Yet the colors just grin and bloom,
Painting the skies to dispel the gloom.

As night falls, fireflies twirl in the air,
Winking at stars with a playful flair.
Nature hums softly, a tune of delight,
In every drop, the world feels light.

Orchard Soliloquy

Trees chat softly, roots intertwined,
'We've got apples, fresh and fine!'
The breeze giggles, messing their hair,
As squirrels debate who's got more flair.

A robin complains of a missing snack,
While a raccoon sneaks up for a quick hack.
Branches shake with laughter so bright,
As berries blush with pure delight.

Old trunks tell tales of sun and shade,
Of silly storms that never stayed.
Lemons roll away with a cheeky grin,
While cherries giggle, hoping to win.

Beneath the stars, the shadows play,
In fruit-laden dreams, they dance and sway.
With every fruit, a story's spun,
In orchard whispers, all is fun.

Citrus Dreams Under Starlit Skies

Orange slices twinkle like tiny stars,
Lemons chat about their little scars.
Limes with zest, full of crazy flair,
Roll their eyes, a fruity affair.

Branches sway with a giggly sway,
As critters gossip about the day.
Grapefruit claps, all zest, no sour,
In moonlit nights, they bloom and flower.

A whisper flows through the citrus trees,
Tickling hearts on a gentle breeze.
With every scent, a chuckle flies,
In the laughter where sweetness lies.

At dawn, they stretch with a citrus grin,
Each seed a wish, where joy begins.
Under starlit skies, the stories unfold,
In laughter's arms, life is gold.

The Glow of Hidden Wonders

Beneath the boughs, a cat in stripes,
Dreaming of uncatchable kites.
An apple rolls, it takes a spin,
While squirrels plot their next big win.

Grapes are giggling, can you hear?
Their juicy gossip, oh so near.
A pear parades with pomp and flair,
While bees agree, it's quite a fair.

The sun winks bright, a cheeky ray,
As birds conspire to steal the day.
Ants march in line, a grand brigade,
In this sweet mess, no dull charade.

Laughter rings from tree to tree,
Nature's jesters, wild and free.
With every rustle, joy ignites,
Under the glow of hidden lights.

Interlude of Fruits and Flowers

Lemons giggle in a row,
Wondering when they'll get to glow.
Bananas slip and trip with glee,
Promising a peel of spree.

Marigolds dance on the breeze,
Whispers floating through the trees.
A plump tomato strikes a pose,
While dandelions, comedy goes.

Raspberries wear their shiny crowns,
Cackling softly, never frowns.
The daisies flirt with tipsy bees,
Creating buzz and swaying leaves.

In this patch, there's no defeat,
Just nature's humor, oh so sweet.
With colors bold and laughter bright,
A merry tale unfolds in light.

Old Trees, New Stories

Beneath the branches, tales collide,
Of critters' plans they can't abide.
Wise old trunks sit and debate,
While the squirrels mock and speculate.

Knots and gnarls hold secrets tight,
A tale of bark and morning light.
A chipmunk scolds the roaming hen,
"Cut it out! This is my glen!"

Leaves trade jokes in rustling laughs,
As shadows play their silly crafts.
An owl hoots with a knowing grin,
"Let's do this dance once again!"

With roots so deep and branches wide,
These giants keep their humor tied.
In every creak, a story spins,
Old trees laugh as new life begins.

Whispered Promises in the Shade

Under the canopy, secrets thrive,
Where echoes of laughter come alive.
A blanket of leaves, a patchwork quilt,
Where whispered dreams and fun are built.

A picnic spread, the ants brigade,
Ready to serve and never fade.
Crumbs of laughter, crumbs of cheer,
All joined in, their mission clear.

The blooms all gossip in soft tones,
A chatter of petals, like playful bones.
With butterflies showing off their flair,
In this shady nook, no room for despair.

Every rustle shares a jest,
In this cozy haven, all are blessed.
Together, the shade and sun collide,
Whispered promises of joy abide.

A Tapestry of Colors

Apples red dance with glee,
Lemons whisper, 'Let's get free!'
Peaches giggle, roll around,
While laughing berries paint the ground.

Greens are plotting with the bees,
Comics shared on rustling leaves.
The carrot jokes are quite a hit,
But onion spies will never quit.

Purple grapes laugh, try to sing,
While orange zest just loves to swing.
Cherries tease with puns so loud,
As nature's court forms quite a crowd.

In this patch of vibrant view,
Every fruit has something new.
With friends all lurking 'neath the tree,
Get ready for a fruit spree!

Nectar and Nostalgia

Buzzing bees in playful flight,
Sip the nectar, what a sight!
Silly flowers shake and sway,
With honey dreams that steal the day.

A blackberry wears a tiny hat,
While strawberries chat with the cat.
Ripe bananas burst with pride,
As goofy pears try to hide.

The melon squad throws a feast,
Cowabunga! The fun won't cease.
Laughing juice drips from the vine,
Each drop a memory so divine.

Juicy bites and laughter mix,
As sweet moments play their tricks.
Embrace the joys from trees so grand,
In every taste, fond memories stand!

The Secret Language of Trees

Whispers low from leafy crowns,
Giggling roots beneath the grounds.
Branches wave like happy arms,
And trunks boast about their charms.

Squirrels share their nutty dreams,
While branches plot, or so it seems.
Bark has tales both old and wise,
As each leaf teases the skies.

Late-night owl debates the lore,
As shadows dance beside the core.
Pine needles snicker at the show,
And vines take selfies, don't you know?

In this circle of delight,
Trees converse till morning light.
With secrets wrapped in bark and green,
They spread their joy, a playful scene!

Sunlit Pathways and Hidden Delights

Down the path where sunbeams play,
Mischievous shadows find their way.
Each flower winks, a sunny smile,
With honeyed scents that beg a while.

Puddles giggle, splash on feet,
While ants march with a steady beat.
Each turn reveals a tasty prize,
With cheeky bugs in disguise.

A hidden nook, what will you find?
A wild berry with love entwined.
The sunbeams wink, 'Come join the fun!'
With laughter growing, everyone!

In nature's game, we seize the day,
To dance through light, to laugh and play.
With every twist, there's joy to greet,
On sunny paths, we can't be beat!

Children of the Grove

Bouncing round like little springs,
Chasing shadows, laughing things.
Apples rolling, giggles fly,
Watch those squirrels! Oh my, oh my!

Sticky fingers, muddy toes,
Pinecone hats and rhubarb bows.
Whispers of hide-and-seek,
Who's the thief, and who's the sneak?

Jumping high to catch a breeze,
Finding treasures 'neath the trees.
Unruly hair and wild delight,
Dancing past the fading light.

Reflections in the Fruit

Mirror, mirror, on the vine,
What's that funny face of mine?
Swollen cheeks of berry juice,
Giggling hard, we let loose!

Bouncing berries, bright and round,
Rolling laughter on the ground.
Lemon lights all fit to burst,
Taste the sweetness, quench the thirst!

Peachy faces, winks and grins,
Crafty plans to sneak a win.
Who can pluck the biggest one?
Under the tree, we're having fun!

The Breath of Blossoms

Petals dancing, swirling round,
Buzzing bees make happy sound.
Hiccups in the springtime air,
Funny sneezes everywhere!

A pollen fight, oh what a sight!
Sneezing friends take off in flight.
Laughter echoes, blossoms sway,
Join the game, come out and play!

Colors tumble, petals cheer,
Giggle fits that we can't clear.
A daisy crown? A fashion dare!
With monarch wings, we float in air.

Moonlight on the Trees

Under the glow, the shadows creep,
Witty owls begin to peep.
Twinkling lights, fireflies zoom,
Chasing laughs around the gloom.

Whispers soft through leaves they tease,
'Who can climb the highest trees?'
Twisting gnomes with cheeky grins,
Shaping dreams like paper winds.

Ghostly branches wave goodnight,
Tickling noses, a hoot of fright.
Mischief brews under the stars,
As the moonlight sings our bars.

Twilight's Fruitful Embrace

Beneath the trees, a fruit parade,
Apples jive while lemons fade.
Peaches giggle, cherries sigh,
As peachy jokes make passersby.

A squirrel dons a tiny hat,
Complains about a lazy cat.
He busts a move, twirls with glee,
As acorns roll, oh what a spree!

The strawberries throw a raucous bash,
While blueberries do the funky flash.
Under the shade, they twist and shout,
Creating laughter roundabout.

As dusk creeps in with a wink,
The fruits all gather for a drink.
They toast to smiles and giggles too,
In the garden, with skies so blue.

Whimsy Amid the Blossoms

Daisies wear their polka dots,
Tulips dancing in their pots.
With bumblebees in quirky flights,
And all the flowers sharing bites.

A daffodil tells corny puns,
While daisies bring the jelly runs.
They play a game of hide and seek,
With laughter echoing, not so meek.

The breeze joins in, a playful tease,
Sways the blooms with gentle ease.
Each petal laughs, a fragrant cheer,
As bees conspire to taste the beer.

So gather 'round, let good times swell,
Among the blossoms, all is well.
In this sprightly, merry land,
Funny antics in flowered strands.

The Orchard's Silent Cry

Under the boughs, a pear takes flight,
It dreams of grapes, what a delight!
With apples plotting sneaky schemes,
While oranges whisper juicy dreams.

A rogue banana starts to sway,
Challenges others to a play.
But watch out for the sneaky bramble,
It giggles loud, ready to scramble.

The moonlight nudges fruits to sing,
Figs and plums embrace the spring.
In silly puns, they share their plight,
As they transform into desserts tonight.

With laughter ripening on each branch,
The fruits compete in a fruity dance.
While whispering vows to always stay,
In this wild and wonky ballet.

Mosaics of Sun and Shade

A single grape rolled down with flair,
Landed on a red raspberry's hair.
They giggled hard, what a scare,
As all the fruits took up the dare.

The kiwi wore a tiny crown,
While the vegetables just frowned.
A carrot dreamed of moonlit skies,
Yet couldn't take the fruit's reprise.

In patches bright with laughter clear,
The watermelon volunteers a cheer.
They pop and bounce, a merry crew,
In this colorful celestial zoo!

And when the stars peek down to see,
The fruits throw parties with wild glee.
With jokes and riddles, night's a game,
In the nature's court, they stake their claim.

Time's Lullaby in Leafy Halls

Underneath the boughs, we giggle,
Chasing shadows with a wiggle.
An apple rolled, a duck did quack,
Who knew fruit could cause such a crack?

Squirrels dance with marbles bright,
Swapping tales from day to night.
The breeze carries laughter wide,
While the tree's trunk tries to hide.

The grass tickles silly feet,
As our games skip to a beat.
Laughter echoes, soft and spry,
Beneath the branches, we all fly.

With each pluck, a battle starts,
Juicy bites, debatable arts.
In this leafy realm so grand,
Funny moments hand in hand.

Tasting Time Beneath the Canopy

Grapes in clusters, hanging tight,
Throw them up! What a sight!
Plucking fruits with silly grace,
Watch them tumble, hit my face!

Peaches giggle, round and sweet,
As we dance on grassy feet.
Every step, a rollicking race,
Nature's funhouse, what a place!

Lemons squint from their high perch,
Think they're sour? They just lurch!
With every laugh that we compile,
The fruits seem to wear a smile!

Beneath the leaves, we sip and munch,
Living it up, it's a fruity lunch.
Time slips by in joyful spree,
Caught in fruit's sweet comedy.

The Gentle Pull of Harvest

Here comes Bob with a big fat sack,
Tumbling down with a hefty clack.
Pumpkins giggle, rolling round,
While golden corn begins to sound.

Tugging at vines, a bumpy ride,
Let's see who can take the slide!
Laughter bursts with each sweet bite,
Harvest games, a pure delight.

Tomatoes ready, oh what fun!
Red and juicy, one by one.
In a race of who can pluck,
Better watch out or you'll get stuck!

With baskets full and hearts so light,
We dance together, what a sight!
The harvest time, a playful cheer,
Each giggle echoes, loud and clear.

A Canvas of Fluttering Leaves

Leaves swirl down like confetti bright,
As we twirl in pure delight.
Whispers soft and tinged with gold,
Watch our antics unfold, behold!

Crisp apples bounce, trying to flee,
Daring us—come catch the spree!
Nature's palette, a wild tease,
Catching colors with the breeze.

We toss leaves up, a frolicsome bunch,
While squirrels scurry to crunch and munch.
With every flutter, a giggle slips,
Wrapping laughter in autumn's grips.

A canvas wide, with colors bold,
Playing in stories yet untold.
In this art, we find our laughs,
Nature's game, with joyful paths.

The Twilight Gatherers

In the evening glow, we gather,
Chasing fireflies that dance like mad.
Our laughter mingles with the shadows,
As the grapes try to hide, oh so glad.

Squeezed between giggles and whispers,
A rogue raccoon steals our prized pie.
He tiptoes off with a cheeky grin,
Inviting us to chase him, oh my!

Under the stars, we craft our tales,
Of the silly things we've done all day.
Nature listens with a winking eye,
As the twilight plays, come what may.

With arms full of fruit, we march home,
Declaring ourselves the kings of the jest.
In the night, playful spirits roam,
For tomorrow's fun, we'll need our rest!

Beneath the Apple's Shade

Here we lie in the cool, green grass,
Surrounded by apples, sweet and round.
A fruit fight breaks; oh, what a splash!
With every hit, more laughter's found.

A squirrel watches, plotting his heist,
He thinks he's sly, but we're quite wise.
We toss him a core; it's our kind's feast,
He scurries away with gleaming eyes.

Picnic blankets blanket the lawn,
As we munch and chitchat, feeling spry.
Jam-covered fingers sticky with fun,
Honey drips, as we howl at the sky.

Beneath green umbrellas, stories grow,
Of the shenanigans too wild to keep.
With seeds of laughter, our friendship blooms,
As the sunset falls, we drift to sleep.

Chasing the Dappled Sun

We race through patches of golden light,
Our shadows mingle in a silly dance.
The daisies giggle at our delight,
As the bluebirds join in for a prance.

Catching sunbeams in our little jars,
We sprinkle them in the pies we bake.
No one can see who's winning this race,
But who really cares, it's all just for sake!

A wandering goat decides to join,
He's come for the fun and the snacks, of course.
With a hop and a skip, he claims a throne,
Laughs erupt as he gallops with force.

Together we sing songs of the day,
Turning mundane into a marvelous bliss.
With every new laugh and goofy play,
We seal our memories with a quirky kiss.

Laughter of the Harvest

In the fields where the pumpkins grow,
We carve silly faces, grinning wide.
Every laugh echoes, stealing the show,
Food flying as we all take a ride!

The scarecrow's hat flies off with a puff,
A gust of wind joins our playful spree.
Chasing it down is terribly tough,
We tumble and roll, as soft as can be.

The corn maze reveals our merry fate,
Lost and giggling, we stumble around.
Trying to navigate turns with no bait,
As the map stays buried in lost and found.

At dusk, we gather in tired delight,
With baskets full, we cheer and we sway.
The laughter we share is our true harvest,
For it fills our hearts, come what may!

Under the Canopy's Embrace

Under wide branches, we hide from the sun,
A squirrel steals apples, think he's so fun.
We chuckle and laugh, as he dances in glee,
    Chasing his tail, thinking he's free.

With lemons he juggles, though they roll away,
His antics so silly, they brighten our day.
We share our own snacks, forgotten we last,
While he takes a bow, our laughter amassed.

The wind it whispers, tickles our cheeks,
While the busy bees chatter, as if they could speak.
We toss them our crumbs, and they seem to cheer,
    In this silly tangle, what's there to fear?

So here's to the moments, silly and light,
Under the green where we laugh with delight.
A squirrel, two friends, a world full of joy,
    In this canopy dance, we all are a toy.

Echoes of Distant Larks

The larks sing sweetly, up high in the trees,
While we chase our shadows, like children with ease.
We trip over roots, laugh at our plight,
Echoes of giggles fill up the twilight.

With each playful note, the sky starts to glow,
We dance with the branches, our spirits in tow.
A butterfly winks, flutters right by,
As we scoop up soft daisies to toss in the sky.

Each pluck from the ground feels like sheer delight,
We crown ourselves kings, in this whimsical night.
With laughter that rises, like bubbles in air,
We twirl like the larks, free without care.

And as day turns to dusk, we kick off our shoes,
The echoes of larks, leave behind their clues.
Tomorrow holds more, for us to explore,
With fun in our hearts, and laughter galore!

Dance of the Orchard Spirits

The spirits come out when the sun starts to fade,
With jests and with giggles, their mischief displayed.
They twirl with the leaves, so sprightly and spry,
With a wink and a chuckle, they flit and they fly.

Footsteps in shadows, they shuffle around,
Messing with apples that tumble to ground.
A fruit here, a fruit there, a comical spree,
As the spirits of laughter bewilder the tree.

They grab at our hats, and they untie our shoes,
With a smile and a giggle, they'll refuse to lose.
In this playful parade, we join in their game,
Each twirl and each tumble, we're never the same.

So come join the dance, let go of your cares,
With spirits beside us, we float through the air.
In the orchard's embrace, we laugh and we sing,
In this merry old dance, let your heart take wing!

Fragrance on the Wind

The breeze carries scents of sweet fruity fun,
As we play hide and seek under the sun.
A cheeky raccoon plots his next escape,
While we giggle and plot our own grand drape.

We chase after strawberries, fresh off the vine,
Bouncing and stumbling, we're feeling so fine.
With baskets in hand, our loot up so high,
We munch on our treasures and wave to the sky.

A sudden loud rustle, what could it be?
The spirits are laughing, don't take it from me!
Ghosts of the orchard are spinning around,
In this fragrant lark, joy knows no bound.

So let's make a toast, to the scents and the sights,
In the playful orchard, where laughter ignites.
With smiles so wide, and hearts full of cheer,
We dance with the breeze, and banish all fear.

Secrets Among the Trees

Whispers from branches, a squirrel's big scheme,
Hiding acorns, while chasing a dream.
All the birds gossip, they chirp and they play,
While the wind rolls in, carrying secrets away.

The apples wear glasses, they look so elite,
Comparing their colors, a subtle retreat.
A pear tells a joke, the peaches all laugh,
While the bananas dance, taking a selfie, half.

A fig is an artist, with juice for a pen,
Painting the sunset for all of her friends.
While the twinkling stars smile back from above,
Nature's odd secrets are shared out of love.

The trees throw a party, with branches all wide,
Hot cider and laughter, their roots open wide.
As the moon hits the stage, and the termites applaud,
Even the owls can't help but nod.

When Petals Fall like Stars

The petals are giggling, floating so light,
Dancing on breezes, it's quite a sight.
Each bloom spins tales, of bees and their chase,
While butterflies twirl, in a flower's embrace.

One daisy claims fame for the best bumblebee,
While tulips have tantrums, so feisty and free.
A rose pricks her ego, "I've got the best scent!"
While dahlias just laugh, "You need someone bent!"

Unlike falling stars, they settle with flair,
Leaving charms on the ground for the squirrels to fair.
Snapping selfies with petals that fell,
Each snap brings forth its own funny story to tell.

As dusk paints the sky, shadows frolic around,
The petals and critters escape from the ground.
In this wild bloom of joy, chaos sets free,
They flutter and spin, just cute as can be.

Nectar of the Afternoon

Sweet sips of sunshine, the bees sing their song,
With flowers all buzzing, they just can't go wrong.
Each flower in line, waiting turns at the cup,
While hummingbirds dive, they won't ever give up.

A wiggly worm wanted a taste of the treat,
He slipped on a petal, oh what a defeat!
With every small stumble, the bees roll their eyes,
While laughter swells up under bright sunny skies.

The ants in a hurry, with snacks on their backs,
Dodge wasps and fondue, doing their acts.
A dance-off erupts, with moves so divine,
Even the ladybugs join in for a shine.

So nectar so sweet brings out all of the reviews,
With silly little stories, and some sticky shoes.
In this sunny affair, no frown can be found,
Just the joy of an afternoon that spins 'round and 'round.

Echoes of Springtime

Daffodils quip, "Tickle us please!"
While crocuses chime in with giggles of tease.
The sun brings warm rays, tickling the air,
While buds try to whisper, but can only share.

The frogs are now croaking a new song of cheer,
As they jump on their thrones, without any fear.
The turtles just chuckle, in a slow-motion race,
While bumblebees boss all the blooms in the place.

Time for a picnic, ants march in line,
With crumbs of delight and some juice that is fine.
As the clouds do a jig, and the wind gives a wink,
Nature's odd humor makes us all think.

Now blossoms are swaying, as laughter takes flight,
In echoes of springtime, everything feels right.
With each burst of color, a snicker, a grin,
We celebrate joy with the season's sweet spin.

Shadows of the Harvest Moon

Under the glowing sphere, we skip,
With a basket full of fruits, a real trip.
The apples giggle, the pears all tease,
While we make silly faces at the buzzing bees.

The pumpkins grin wide, 'We're here for the show!'
As we dance like fools, with our heads all aglow.
A scarecrow rolls his eyes, he's seen better days,
While the corn stalks whisper in hilarious ways.

We stumble and trip, fall into the heap,
Giggling like children, we can't seem to leap.
As we munch on the harvest, bit by bit,
Who knew that squash could be such a hit?

With laughter as loud as the crows in the air,
We crunch through the leaves, without a single care.
The harvest moon beams, it can't help but smile,
As we sip on our cider, staying for a while.

Petals Dance on the Breeze

The petals twirl like a clumsy ballet,
While butterflies snicker and flutter away.
A bee in a tux, with a top hat so neat,
Dances in circles, quite light on his feet.

The daisies gossip, sharing what's new,
'Did you see that squirrel? It's sporting a shoe!'
The roses just blush, they can't quite keep still,
While the tulips all laugh; they think it's a thrill.

A wind gust arrives, with jokes held inside,
The daisies crack up, they're all filled with pride.
As daisies plop down like they're rolling a dice,
The laughter erupts, oh, wouldn't that be nice?

Then comes a cat, all fluff and no grace,
Chasing the petals that dance all over the place.
The flowers all cheer, it's a humorous sight,
As petals spin freely in the softening light.

The Sweetness of Ripened Days

In fields of gold, where the fruit's ripe and round,
We trip over vines, fall flat on the ground.
With berries that giggle, we munch and we munch,
Getting sticky and sweet; it's a delightful brunch!

The sun shines bright, making juice of our cheeks,
While quirky old chickens redefine what 'sneaks.'
Oh look, there's a melon, it's rolling away,
Chasing us down, like it's got a say!

With laughter as sweet as sugar on toast,
We'll toast to the fruits, our funny host.
Banana peels slip, and we're down for the count,
Rolling like apples, oh, what a discount!

Later we giggle, with laughter so loud,
Making funny faces, we draw quite a crowd.
Harvesting joy in each juicy bite,
Turning simple days into pure delight.

Echoes of Forgotten Seasons

Back in the day, when the days were all bright,
We chased after shadows, from morning to night.
Old socks as our shoes, we danced in the dirt,
Finding old treasures and feeling quite pert.

The sunsets sang songs of each season gone by,
While acorns would tumble, like stars in the sky.
The pine trees would chuckle, their needles all sharp,
As we pretended to play a tune on a harp.

There's laughter in wind, like secrets and quips,
The crickets applaud with their rhythmic little flips.
Old leaves gave a cheer, as they twirled in the air,
Reminding us all of how silly we dare.

So raise up a toast, to the fun and the plays,
To the echoes of laughter from those hidden days.
With a wink to the past, we continue our roam,
In the joyful embrace of our childhood home.

Essence of the Ripened

The apples giggle on the trees,
Hiding from the buzzing bees.
They bounce and sway with cheeky pride,
Wishing to take a playful ride.

Bananas peek from leafy wraps,
Wearing smiles, avoiding mishaps.
Lemons pucker, making faces,
While cherries dance in fruity races.

Peaches whisper silly dreams,
Of ice cream sundaes with whipped cream.
But when the harvest time is here,
They laugh and shout, "Let's volunteer!"

So gather 'round, let's pluck a few,
For fruit salad, a jolly crew.
As laughter ripens in the sun,
These fruits are waiting just for fun!

Soft Hues of Dusk

The twilight paints the sky so bright,
With oranges and pinks in flight.
The berries blush, all shy and sweet,
As crickets tap their little feet.

A plum rolls down with quite a thud,
Splattering puddles of purple mud.
The nightfall giggles, stars appear,
As fruit insists, "Let's grab a beer!"

Peaches glow like lanterns dim,
While watermelon sings a hymn.
With every shade, the fruit takes flight,
In dusk's embrace, they share delight.

So bring some bowls to catch the cheer,
And dance with fruit, let's raise a beer!
As night unfolds in laughter's scheme,
We'll feast in colors, like a dream!

Ties of Earth and Sky

The pumpkin jokes are sure to land,
With goofy grins, they make a stand.
Tomatoes giggle, rolling free,
While carrots chase them 'round the tree.

The clouds send whispers to the ground,
In puddles, sticky fruit is found.
With raindrops rattle and pop around,
The harvest sings a silly sound.

The sun throws rays like golden darts,
While veggies do their funny parts.
They form a band, a veggie choir,
Playing tunes that'll never tire.

So let's embrace this wacky show,
With every fruit and veggie glow.
In nature's folly, give a cheer,
For all our friends, who gather here!

The Song of Sweet Abundance

A bunch of grapes begins to sway,
Singing jokes in bold array.
"Hey, can we grape this whole delight?
Let's dance together through the night!"

Pineapples wear their crowns with flair,
As bananas slide without a care.
They sing a tune of tangy glee,
In juicy chorus, wild and free.

Strawberries tease with polka dots,
While figs share secrets in sweet thoughts.
The orchard buzzes with a hum,
While fruit and laughter swirl and drum.

So gather 'round and join the fun,
For fruity joy has just begun.
With every bite, we'll sing and cheer,
For fruit is life, let's bring it near!

Beneath the Branches' Embrace

A squirrel stole my sandwich, quite bold,
He chattered with glee, his story told.
I offered him chips, a tasty delight,
He danced on the branch, what a silly sight!

The apples all giggled, they swayed to and fro,
They watched as I chased him, all puffed out, though.
The bees buzzed my tune, like a choir of bees,
As I tripped on a root and fell with a wheeze.

The shadows grew long, my laughter took flight,
The dog joined the chase, barking with all might.
Around the tall trees, we spun in a spin,
A party for critters, oh, what a win!

With snacks in the grass, all the friends came around,
We feasted together, munching joyously, sound.
In the daylight's end, under twilight's embrace,
I found that my heart held a warmer place.

Sighs of a Summer's End

The sun gave a wink, a cheeky good-bye,
As I donned my hat, all the bugs chose to fly.
With grass on my knees and a red stain I found,
I chuckled at how summer flipped upside down.

The pumpkins were grinning, all plump and round,
While melons were laughing, lost on the ground.
"Is it too late to tan?" one ripe peach moaned,
As the clouds started gathering, his sorrow now honed.

A bird took a dive, stole my cookie, so sly,
I gasped at his speed, as he soared through the sky.
With whispers of fall in the rustling trees,
I waved to the breeze, stifled giggles with ease.

I learned from the garden, each age has its tune,
With laughter blooming 'neath the harvest moon.
So here's to the season, let us give a cheer,
For fun in the sun and all of its dear!

Orchard Serenade

The winds played a tune, so whimsical, bright,
While apples all jiggled, what a playful sight!
A worm wrote a ballad, all mushy and sweet,
About loving the leaves and a wild dancing beet!

The sunbeams performed, as peaches took stage,
Each fruit had a story, their laughter a rage.
I clapped on the grass, as the show went along,
When a tomato threw shade, knowing he was wrong.

The figs decided to hop, try a jig,
While pears wore a hat, feeling spry and big.
In this merry orchard, the air was alive,
As friends all celebrated, we knew we'd survive.

So raise up your cups, filled with cider and cheer,
And dance with the fruits, there's no sorrow here!
With echoes of laughter that reach the blue sky,
We'll bask in this joy, never asking why.

The Quiet Joy of Roots

The roots had a meeting, all tangled and tight,
Whispered secrets of soil through the moonlit night.
With laughter that bubbled up through all the dirt,
They shared tales of spills, of fruits and of hurt.

A blushing tomato, who tried to grow tall,
Declared he had tripped over one wayward wall.
The carrots all snickered, their greens in a bunch,
While onions just laughed, with a tear in their punch.

"Let's dig a nice groove!" yelled a radish in glee,
"Let's sway with the grasses, and dance with the bee!"
With roots intertwined, they all found their song,
In harmony rich, where all voices belong.

So next time you wander through rows down below,
Remember the roots and their whimsical flow.
For joy can be quiet, yet bubbling with cheer,
In the heart of the garden, the laughter is clear!

Where Blossoms Dream

In a place where fruits take naps,
Bees wear tiny, funny hats.
Where trees hold meetings by the creek,
And chirping birds play hide and seek.

The apples laugh while hanging high,
Telling stories as they sigh.
Cherries giggle, bright and round,
Waiting for their laughs to sound.

With squirrels playing tag at dusk,
They share their snacks from golden husk.
As shadows dance and moments freeze,
Nature's jokes float on the breeze.

So come and join this merry spree,
Where laughter grows on every tree.
In this land, you'll find your theme,
Where blossoms smile and nature beams.

The Dance of Ripening

The fruits are practicing their dance,
With wobbly moves, they take a chance.
Bananas twirl with a cheerful wink,
As pumpkins ponder, "Do we stink?"

The grapes form rows for a parade,
Twirling under the sun's cascade.
Plums throw confetti in the air,
While pears declare, "We don't care!"

Lemons laugh with zesty zeal,
Squeezing jokes like juice to feel.
As cherries burst in fits of cheer,
Each ripple sings, "The end is near!"

So watch them prance, so bright and bold,
Each fruity story just unfolds.
A jolly show with every seam,
A dance of ripening, sweet dream.

Golden Hues and Gentle Breezes

Golden rays tickle the leaves,
As birds are wearing their finest weaves.
Butterflies whisper tiny tales,
While sunlight dances, never fails.

Lemons swing in the midst of cheer,
Chortling at folks who come near.
The daffodils nod in delight,
Teasing the daisies through the night.

Winds tickle each branch and sway,
Rustling secrets of the day.
Fruit-flavored giggles burst through air,
Making everyone feel they care.

So come enjoy this sunny tease,
Where golden hues mix with the breeze.
Here laughter blooms, a wild spree,
Nature's humor sets us free.

A Symphony of Leaves

Leaves play music in the sun,
Chatting loudly, oh what fun!
Rustling whispers, soft and sweet,
Nature's laughter dances at our feet.

Acorns bouncing, squirrels trip,
In their hats, they take a sip.
While breezes play the flute so fine,
And all join in, a grand design.

Glimmers fly as shadows sway,
Whimsical notes lead the way.
Stems are laughing, branches cheer,
Life's a concert, come draw near!

Join this jam of colors bright,
Where harmony meets pure delight.
A symphony that never leaves,
Crafted by the heart of eaves.